Windcatcher

Windcatcher

New and Selected Poems
1964–2006

Breyten Breytenbach

Harcourt, Inc.
Orlando Austin New York San Diego London

www.HarcourtBooks.com

Library of Congress Cataloging-in-Publication Data
Breytenbach, Breyten.
Windcatcher: new and selected poems, 1964–2006/
Breyten Breytenbach.—1st ed.
p.   cm.
I. Title.
PR9369.3.B67W56   2007
821'.914—dc22   2007009164
ISBN 978-0-15-101532-0

Text set in Bembo
Designed by Kaelin Chapell Broaddus

Printed in the United States of America
First edition
K J I H G F E D C B A

For Yolande and for Daphnée

Contents

2. The Undanced Dance

(Poems from Prison, 1975–1982)

*Through the empty arch comes a wind, a mental wind
blowing relentlessly over the heads of the dead, in search
of new landscapes and unknown accents; a wind that smells
of baby's spittle, crushed grass, and jellyfish veil, announcing
the constant baptism of newly created things.*

—Federico García Lorca, *In Search of Duende*

Windcatcher

Iron Cow Blues
(Poems in Exile, 1964–1975)

like this, the blowfly
in a high wooden tower;
like this, the iceberg full of ants

—Jan Afrika

threat of the sick
For B. Breytenbach

Ladies and gentlemen,
let me introduce you to Breyten Breytenbach,
the thin man in the green sweater; he is pious
and holds and hammers his long-drawn head
to fabricate a poem for you, as for example:

I'm scared to close my eyes
I don't wish to live in the dark *and still see* what passes
the hospitals of Paris are crammed with pale people
standing at windows to make obscene gesticulations
like the angels in the furnace
the streets are flayed and slippery with rain

my eyes are starched
they/you will bury me on a day as soaked as this
when sods are raw black flesh
and wetness snaps and stains leaves and jaded flowers
before light can gnaw at them a sky sweats white blood,
but I shall refuse to paint out my eyes

rip off my bony wings
the mouth is too intimate not to feel pain
put on boots for my funeral so I may hear
mud kissing your feet
sparrows droop their shiny leaking heads blossom-black
on the green sleeves of muttering monk trees

plant me in a hill near a dam with snapdragons
let cunning bitter ducks crap cravings on my grave
in the rain the souls of crazed women slyly invade cats,
fears and fears and fears with drenched colorless heads
and I shall neither hold nor soothe this black tongue ...

But look, he is harmless. Do have mercy on him

report

I saw couples kissing in doorways
turning around with open mouths I walked
across bridges and heard people cough below
I saw grayheads riding in taxis
look through rain-thick windows at buildings
no longer there. snow in winter
and grapes in the summer but I
don't remember much about it

I saw the midnight sun
and birds of all sizes and fish
in the water and the southern cross above a peak
and cats wearing boots and drunken women
and bare trees with blossoms.
snow in the winter
and grapes in summer but
I don't remember much about it

I too heard roosters crow
and the call of trains and voices
in my bed and gods on the roof and I saw
dragons in zoos and the beards
of friends and smelled the sun.
snow in winter and grapes in summer
but I don't remember much about it

death sets in at the feet

One should simply doze off
yet they say for 48 hours consciousness will
still beat at the steamed-up windows of the skull
    like a fish in a basket
      or an astronaut in his spacetub beyond control
      or a Jew under a pyramid of Jews
      or a nigger(lover) in a cell
with a prickling of pins that begins in the soles.

Could it be thus?
The giddiness as the floor tilts
and a membrane of water draws over trees
and a zealous hand embraces the throat more tightly?
And what a farce, this fumbling for pictures.

Last week's chrysanthemums are already rotten
on their stems, the green veins perished rubber tubes,
they who were yakking parrots
are now drooping withered wings.

Yesterday's white carnations stink like slumped old women.
Yesterday's red roses have a deeper bloom
as smothered fists.

People usually die flat on their backs,
feet coldly erect as petrified rabbits
or blossoms on a branch,
with a prickling of pins that begins in the soles.

My feet are recalcitrant: I must cajole them,
swaddled in rags, because I'm not yet done,
must still learn how to die,
I must still decide how to make up my mind.

For now I gaze through a mirror into a riddle,
but tomorrow it will be from face to face.

rebel song

give me a pen
so I may sing
that life is not in vain

give me a season
an autumn a spring
to see sky with open eyes
when the peach tree vomits its white plenitude
a tyranny will be brought to earth

let mothers lament
may breasts become dry
and wombs shrivel
when the scaffold finally weans its own

give me that love
which won't rot between fingers,
give me a love like this love I must give you,
my dove

grant me a heart
that will pulsate its throb
more strongly than the white thrashing
heart of a terrified dove in the dark
knock louder than bitter bullets

give me a heart
small fountain of blood
to spout blossoms of bliss
for blood is never for naught

I need to die before I'm dead
when my heart is still fertile and red
before I eat the darkened soil of doubt

give me two lips
and bright ink for tongue
to write the earth
one vast love letter
swollen with the milk of mercy

sweeter day by day
spilling all bitterness
burning as summer
burns sweeter

then let it be summer
without blindfolds or ravens
allow the gallows to give the peach tree
its red fruit of satisfaction

and grant me a love song
of doves of atonement
so I may sing my life was not in vain

for as I die
to wide eyes
under sky
my red song will not lie
my red song will never die

the black city

keep away especially from bitterness, black child,
this and that you're not allowed to dream;
take care not to choke on redeyes,
that your body not become thick and rancid from bile
cruising constantly through phosphorous veins;
better to regularly snip and comb your pawpaw tree
and remember the clouds perform for you too
and rats eat rubbish

I wish to remember a black city, black child
where you may swell with somber light;
seagulls dance like red balloons above the beach
so that you as well may laugh and exult,
caress the water and build towns of sand,
also run up and down a hundred jokes

watch out particularly for the slimy black pawpaw
of bitterness, black child,
he who eats of it dies on bayonets
and in libraries,
will die all alone in the mouth

look, over the sea a sun is born
with a right hand and a left hand,
and he will be black,
as warm and as black as the tickle-throat of the cock

departure

for Du Fu

In the basin between mainland and island lies the sea
within her twilight womb unknown pinnacles and forests
   and valleys
and blackfish and cities and urns of wine and skeletons
   plucked bare
over which the track of our boat streaks
like the flight of a high strange staggering bird.
As I move forward, so the land changes face
above the coast—the terraced fertile slopes
under colorless mountain peaks are the lush bodies of arid
   heads
and bushes will be somber this late in summer.
Now and then, as when one wipes layers of dust and varnish
from an old painting,
a timeless chalked village glimmers through, its cupolas
and towers with banners—lovely, but I still remain
                      a stranger here—
glimmer and fade like the closing of a sleepy bird's
shining eye.
Foam spurts past the plunging bow.
I turn around,
wind folds the sea's features into old lines of passing.
Already the island of our bliss slips a veil of mist over itself:

Since the oldest days there have always been travelers,
so why be sad?

isla negra
(fragmented remains of a lament)

. . . a few pines, straight like pens . . .
clouds smoking along the seams of the sky . . .
in the wind's stitching an ocean lies
frothing with exclamation marks . . .
the island . . . a hole in the water

yesterday today tomorrow

your city as well: and rain turns up
waving columns of gray comrades through the streets
(the wounded animal tears at its own entrails)

bridegroom: you (which you?)

a cap lopsided over one eye
white tendril of smoke from the lips
and a flower in the buttonhole
for today you will wed the earth, *hermano*
today we hand you over to your family-in-time

a few bloodred wreaths
like workers' banners cover the coffin

. . .

we followed your death from day to day, Neruda . . .
you who walked so far to come to the edge of the earth
(was it heaven? was it hell?)

through the torn open streets of Granada
where Lorca lies with bullets seeding his body . . .
past the gray children of Barcelona
and maggot-infested animals
always toward the border
with Spain in your heart . . .
from ancient yet live civilizations with the pulsation
of stone and metal in your veins . . .
over mountain peaks of the Andes
over the sun's altars
toward the dawning of a new and more humane day . . .
under yankee planes of annihilation
through the rotted bitter black rice fields of Vietnam . . .
forward, always forward
together with worker and farm laborer . . .
through the avenues of your poems

AND SUDDENLY THE EARTH WAS ON FIRE

and this great people said: enough!
and stood up, and walked . . .

. . .

we followed your death on foot, Neruda . . .
the rain a funeral train . . . in your beloved city
Santiago, Santiago the radiant lover
of that *other* America
of the proletariat . . .
where tanks now swarm through the streets

where voices of the tortured scream behind walls
where the sun is salty and red

we, too, know *them*—the generals and the bankers
with their manicured fingernails and odoriferous orifices,
the midnight soldiers cursing down doors with gun butts
who scream as they riffle through books
to tear out the small flames of knowledge, freedom,
dignity, and pride,
to cut the stems—
miserable fools—as if bayonets
could spear stars . . .

in our warm climate they also breed in the shadows—
the respectable psychopaths who torture and kill
under cover of "security,"
watchdogs of the exploiters,
the dollar addicts and the blackmailers,
sad gorillas with their chewing-gum minds
and penciled mustaches and dark glasses,
the wiretaps and the microphones
like cockroaches in cranny and nook

we heard how Allende gave his life,
we heard of his contorted body
wrapped in the flag . . .
the reddening flag . . .
upright in the presidential chair . . .
and blood in the streets, on the walls:

the rise and fall of a thousand years
shall not wipe out the footsteps of those killed here

and you are dead:

. . .

a thousand years of walking up and down
will not efface the footsteps
of those who fell here in battle

for when a poet dies
his breath whitens the mirror

you are dead, Neruda,
and with your passing begins our last conversation . . .
what does it matter that your mouth is full of dirt?
words too are but clods
to be thrown in the grave
for words don't grow
but explode softly in black holes of absence
in the terra firma of the dream,
and we remain

to talk to piss to shit

FREEDOM OR DEATH

. . .

...a few black pines like pens ...
the grave a mirror ...
bridegroom, you, flesh-and-breath you,
and the ocean silent as the earth

yesterday was too soon
tomorrow will be too late

FREEDOM OR DEATH
LIBERTAD O MUERTE
DEATH AND LOVE

now you lie in your coffin
as if too big to be boxed in,
the face—how to put it?—anguished,
with the distorted features
of a child alone in a dark room
"Open up! open up! I can't breathe!"

while alive, was the child not alone
in the big room of a body of so many years,
ponderous and gracious like the salamander
with a voice the sound of cracked reeds?
except at times
when your mouth filled with the good clods of Castile
and sometimes lightning flashed from your lips
and sometimes your syllables were a caressing rain,
enjambments of rain over pale hillsides of the woman,
the times of her time when you were voice only,
before your face fattened again into an ancient Aztec,

a pasha, a plutocrat,
a spokesperson, a poet
alone now below the lidded silence of that glass

garlands on the coffin and torn books in the house

(dogs had to foul the shadows, ambassador,
for your death was beyond their understanding,
the voice slipped through their fingers,
so they came to string the sounds on bayonets . . .
but words are cadavers
voice is of the wind in the trees at night
do they not know you cannot spear the heart?)

with cudgels the soldiers around the cemetery
will try to stop the dead from escaping

and in procession, look, from the streets of hovels
in barrios of poverty, look: workers
with their wives and children and friends,
companions and political refugees will come . . .

. . . the "Internationale" . . .
"Rise up, ye damned of the earth . . .
for it is the final fight . . ."

. . .

you are dead, *hermano,*
but come see how death stalks the streets,
come see the cadavers,

come look at the corpses in mirrors of blood,
at faces covered by stale newspapers
that do not dare give the news
which eyes on stalks anyway cannot read

come see the dogs afraid but emboldened
   —by hunger, by hunger—
slouching from gray morning, hungry and skittish
   —from hunger, from hunger—
to whimper as they wolf the leavings
of the dream of socialism.
yankee and soldier are the guardian angels
of the curs of Santiago . . .

come see the flies and the dust and the steel

open your eyes, Neruda:
                    come weep for your people

eavesdropper

you want to know what it is like to live in exile, friend—
what shall I say?
that I'm too young for bitter revolt
and too old for wisdom or resignation
to my Fate?
that I'm only one of many—
the outsiders
the host of outcasts, outlaws,
citizens of the guts of the dark,
one of those "French with a speech defect"
or even that I feel at home here?

yes, but also that I've come to recognize rooms of loneliness,
the soiling of dreams, the remains of memories,
thin wailing of the violin
where eyes turn away to look ever further,
ears mouse-quietly listen inward—
that like a beggar I pray for alms of "news from home,"
the mercy of "do you remember,"
the redemption of "one of these days"?

and that I cannot recall
for songs have died away
to say nothing of faces,
all dreams have been dreamt,
    and as in search for love in the seaweed hair of woman
one abandons oneself in the shuffling anonymous mass
of revolutionaries aged before their time,
of poets without language and blind painters,

of letters without tidings like seas without tides,
of those who choke in the senility of longing
for spirits conjured from incense
to evoke the landscapes of the tongue—
to vomit all knowledge of the self?

shall I provide a deeper meaning then?
that all of us are exiles from Death,
waiting for the call soon to go "home"?

no, for now, groping with leprous hands
I begin to feel those
who were here before us
and all I ask you
in the name
of that
which you want to know
is to be merciful to those who follow us

—*Paris, Easter, 1968*

there's a large sort of bird my love

there's a large sort of bird my love
I don't know if it's a wild goose
or a tame albatross
or maybe a mountain hawk love
immense and light as that snowcapped peak

the breast and belly of the bird are black
so you won't see it fly at night
but it sings with the same high sounds as the stars
and wings of the bird are blue
so by day you can't see how it soars upside-down

sometimes only two fugitive shadows
pass like hands over your eyes my love

pale is the color of my love
black she is in all of my night
and always between me and my eyes

exile, representative
for F.M. and M.K.

you grow less agile, more compliant,
fat squats in your body
like ants deep inside a dead animal,
one day it consumes you,
your eyes burn brighter with solitude

you live as if you'd never die
because you don't exist here
and yet death walks in your body,
down through your intestines
death is knotted in your wings

the earth caves in behind your eyes,
the hills grow still, the emptiness green,
your hands and smile collapse,
photographs and pamphlets are pasted
over memories: *experience is a dream*

you learn to beg
and ply with the raw contrition of your people
the insatiable bureaucrats,
the Officials of World Conscience: you look
through the holes of their hearts into the mirror

with daylight you're still awake,
your mouth gray from muttering;
words swarm like parasites around your tongue
and make nests in your throat

in a crowd you're always a fugitive,
don't smoke, don't drink:
is your life not a weapon?
you go down poisoned with despair,
shot like a dog in a dead-end street

and by the time you want to crack the day's skull
and shout: Look, my people are on their feet!
here comes the mother explosion! *power!*
you've forgotten the silences of language
so that ants will crawl from the cry
belched from your entrails: blind freedom fighters

asylum
para el "C"

I.

first those closest shot holes in you
and the sly night spider
he who waits in every corner of every room
bled through these red doors of daybreak
and the trail of shimmering gossamer choked your veins

blood seeps forever into the ground
the broken body lies, obscenely
raped, in a manger, in a stable
the lips drawn—to grin a last "good-bye"?
teeth are a trampled gate
a broken-down wall
the eyes are open but there's nothing to see
small sentry boxes of an uninhabited realm
two bees petrified in honey and in light
breath shudders somewhere far among birds in trees
and the corpse is already embalmed
with the erotic perfume of decay—

you will be a web of dazzling bones . . .

come, close up the orifices again
please make this body breath-tight
and spin a veil before our eyes
so we may never see how dies the hero
how mortals contemplate the secrets of his carcass

2.

the journey in the land of the lonely
is a route without hostels through a land without borders
all along a sea without shores
with only love as beacon

in the land of the blind all colors are fantastic
each sound bears witness
to the silver language of the mute
with only love as darkness

with only love as fire tower
a barrier against the sea
of notes in a throat where foam
must break open
like a machine gun's whispered message
stuttered in code by the mute
in the ears of the deaf
who can write it down for the blind
with only love as ink

for the machine gun breathes the secret
to reveal all secrets
the machine gun enlightens the way
and washes your feet
and places before you the bread and the wine
so you may come home
with only love as the body of your death

not with the pen but the machine gun

What could I tell you Johnny-Jesus of Nazareth
I white African featherless fowl
I never naked
how should I lay my barren land upon your mind
you who have also foretold your trail
in whose fate dwell skulls grimacing in incense
for whose sake the crucified toll in the winds of hills
worse: in whose name those of the night
are webbed in the spittle of the spider's arse
I'm talking of course of order and civilization?

Should I tell of
hospital beds where experiments are performed on children
every season the wheat is reaped anew
pale cadavers sucking the dark heart in the agony of death
red poppies are swaying on the slopes
the outsider splintered in every mirror
the summer honey tastes of lavender
a black walls himself off in the bitterness of his own shack
the fingerling body of the cicada is green
sun-singers do not know of the black man
the white man knows only the sun
knows nothing about either black or man
what would the black man know of cicadas
and what should I tell the black man about you

Of humility Manjack of Nazareth
of what humility
except that I will not ever really know

nor be allowed to say again
that this cup must be taken from me
the humbleness
not to disown but to despise
not to betray but to annihilate
and to write in white on white
King of the Jews and the Kaffirs and baboons

Shall I then humbly Jesusjohn Man of Nazareth
inherit this fertile carcass of the world
I white African featherless fowl
I never disarmed never bare
I as black as an unuttered verb
of coming and becoming

flame

the fly cannot alight on the lion's blood:
the fire;
the lady's veil rustles with desire:
a flame
born of fire erupts to lap around the lips of the universe,
blinding and terrible
breaks through the brushwood
to split each tree from its black double,
scorches the white worms from the eyes:
sunrise over Africa

I see
neither visions nor revelations, but recognitions:
I seek this place; our silver jet beats above its shadow
like a watch hand over undeciphered scratches of time,
crossing dwellings, the sand snake Nile passes below
and fire captures the sky

in Khartoum the wind is the desert's bloody breath:
"Above, through a sky terrible in its stainless beauty,"
(flames leave no blemish) "and the splendors
of a pitiless blinding glare" (the eye's gaze makes no imprint)
"the simoom caresses you like a lion
with a flaming breath . . .
the very skeletons of mountains . . ." etc.
Sir Richard Burton

Gordon Pasha's consumed head fruits on a spear:
teeth white with grinning clenched against the light,

teeth blackened by the fire's countenance and the tongue's
    ash—
vengeance burns clean—
while the Mahdi's men
in flickering turbans
diminish like corpses across the flats

southward the Kabaka's wives squat
fat on beestings, belching in huts;
further south giraffes gallop gracefully
hoisting bundles of kindling in haste,
and high against slopes of the mountains of fire
where the hoar snow grows
lies the coal black body of the leopard

Africa, so often pillaged, purified, burned!
Africa lives in the sign of fire and flame . . .

letter to butcher from abroad
for Balthazar

the prisoner says
now I'm not sure
whether the sweet Lord roared
but a first fly is dancing
droning against the panes
a blossom tossed against the sky
the walls glisten with blood
one's heart hangs still
for fear this ecstasy might ebb
one gathers the minute bewilderments
as food for the journey of the ungainly gray human
squatting incarcerated in the body

the prisoner states
Li Changyin warned against holes for the rain
Never let your heart unfold with the flowers of spring
One inch of love is an inch of ashes
I hope you will pick out my gray bones
in the blown fires of the earth

as for me, I'll set out on a trip
I'll lie inside my body on the upper deck
to feel the tremors of the boat in my flesh
the ropes dozing all prepared in cool places
the mast will swing for direction against the blue
the sea will stir the sea will smell
the sea will be alive with dolphins
gulls will come to swarm above the heart

and then it will all be silenced to light
as sun with the sounds of a language
rapes each fiber grain and cell—
but I, I will go on a voyage

the prisoner confesses
when your dreams are finally crushed
and you await night's darkening far from your people
like the pine tree painfully yearning for a blaze of sails
its lament shuddering a white wind in the forest
to crouch on Monday mornings crippled like a crow
at the lips of the ocean
then one is ready
to tremble in the soil
and feed the insects
with confessed declarations

I can testify
I can describe the colors from within
the walls are black the snot is gold
blood and pus are ice cream and berry juice
outside against the bulwarks the bird pecks and pecks

I stand on bricks before my fellow man
I am the statue of liberation
with electrodes tied to my balls
I try to scream light into this obscurity
while writing slogans in crimson urine
across my skin over the floor

throttled by the ropes of my guts
I slip on a bar of soap and break my neck
kill myself with the evening paper
tumble from the tenth floor of heaven
to redemption on a street among people

and you, butcher
burdened with the security of the state
what are your thoughts when night begins to show her
    skeleton
and the first burbling scream is forced
from the inmate
as if of birth
flooded by the fluids of parturition?
are you then humbled by this blood-smeared thing
with its humanoid shuddering shocks
and its broken breath of dying
in your hands?
does the heart also tighten in your throat
when you paw its slippery limbs
with the very hands that will caress the secrets of your wife?

tell me, butcher
so that the obstetrics you're made to perform
in the name of my survival
may be revealed to me
in my own tongue

the prisoner says
I don't want to die here

I want to be hanged outside in the desert
with my heart turned toward dawn's cold
where the mountains are flies gorging themselves on the
    horizon
where sand burns with one million silver tongues
and the moon as rotten as a shipwreck
sinks through blue smoke

now tell me, butcher
before that thing becomes a curse
and you may plead only by mouths
of graves
before the risen prisoners of Africa

prayer
in memory of J.K.

Our mild God of all that's sweet and beautiful
Let thy name be always stored in us and therefore hallowed.
Let the republic now come about.
Let others shoot away their will—
Let go! Let go!
So that we too may have a say,
A say like a sea
Around the coasts of our heavenly Still Mountain

Give that we today may earn our daily bread
And the butter, the jam, the wine, the silence,
The silence of wine.
And lead us into temptations of manifold kinds
So that love may jump from body to body
The way flames of being from peak to peak
Bring brambles of fire to the whitest moon

But let us deliver ourselves from evil
So that we may settle the score of centuries
Of stored exploitation, plunder, and treachery,
And the last capitalist dies, poisoned by loot

For ours are the kingdom, the power, and the glory,
For ever and ever and just as eternal
As the shadows and the frontier passages of man
When godlike he tears the earth from heaven

Ay man! Ay man! Ay man!

winter solace

and when it is summer again
we will go walk under the pergola
during the long-legged evenings
to wave to one another

and when darkness then falls
clamber onto the toothed roof
with lanterns like dragon eyes in our hands
to look at the growling moon

and thighs astride the ridge
sit and elucidate
life's secrets whisperingly
like gesticulating Chinese sages

(please don't mope over winter rains)

Dar es Salaam: Harbor of Peace

Dar es Salaam: it is when night is at its deepest
just before morning that the muezzin calls the faithful
for they are still asleep
and his sad cry drifts over index fingers of minarets
    rooftops and lovers and flowers and docks
his sad cry dawns over the city

one proverb goes: "the cock that crows at night
                without waiting for daybreak
should be slaughtered forthwith because it brings
    misfortune";
but a second one states: "it is not wise to react
when called only once in the heart of the night"

you can let that bird go as often as the sun
and it always returns—
I think of you, brothers in exile, with only bitterness for earth

day comes to dig this sweet earth: a sea full of ships and coral
and shells so young they're still all white—beaches
and coconut palms very proud and slender with small firm
    tits,
banana plantations, mangoes, pawpaws;
the city has sparkling clouds and crows weep in the wind,
"caw! caw!" the wind-polished white-breasts predict;
other birds whistle through their wings: "to whistle," so the
    saying goes,
"is to summon the devil"
under office fans the bureaucrats sit

with blistered lips and flies on their hands:
"to wash clothes without water causes poverty"

I think of you, freedom fighters, sick with the paltry vomit
                    of a present you cannot stomach,
armed and frightened on some imprecise border—
"if a man bites you and you rub chickenshit into the wound
his teeth will rot"

with low tide and sundown the Indians come down to the
    sea,
when the moon is a pale conch glistening in creases of the
    void
and stars also swim,
to gossip, smell the low water and twilight,
sit cross-legged and grow still
and when it is dark
seek an India far across the waves

I think of you, exiled brothers in our movement for freedom
trying to follow the sun:
"if you point at the new moon
your finger will be cut, but that finger
should not be confused with the moon,
and if you blow over your pustules in that direction
then it is the moon that fills with pus"

I have heard: "he who eats chicken feet will become a
    vagabond"
"walking bareheaded under the moon will dry up the brain

and one day you will be addled"
"a fool who always enjoys his meals
will never regain understanding"

Ukichomeka kisu ndani ya ala anaposema mwenye
kigugumizi basi hataweza kuendelea na kusema tena:
"stick a knife in its sheath while the stutterer is still talking
and you cut off all his speech"
here night already falls over Dar es Salaam

I will die and go to my father

I will die and go to my father
to Wellington on long legs
gleaming in the light
where rooms are heavy and dark
where stars perch like gulls on the roof
and angels dig for worms in the garden,
I will die and hit the road
   with just a few things
across the Wellington mountains
through the trees and the twilight
and go to my father

the sun will throb in the earth
wind's surf will creak the joints
we will hear the tenants'
scraping feet overhead,
we'll play checkers on the back porch—
what a cheat you are, old man—
and listen on the radio
to news from the night

friends, companions in dying,
don't balk; now life still hangs
like flesh from our bodies
but death won't let us down;
our coming and our going
is like water from the tap
or sounds born in the mouth

just like coming and going;
our skeletons will *know* freedom

come with me
                in my dying—going to my father
to Wellington where angels
with worms fish fat stars from heaven;
let's die and perish and be merry:
my father has a big boardinghouse

in a burning sea

how often were we wrapped in coolness on the floor
the smell of turpentine and fire
the canvases white to our empty eyes
night's indifference
and the moon a smile somewhere outside
out of sight
days decompose like seasons beyond the panes
leaves of rain, a face, a cloud, this poem
I wanted to leave my imprint on you
to brand you with the flaming hour
of being alone
no fire sings as clear
as the silver ashes of your movements
and your melancholy body
I wanted to draw that sadness from you
so that you might be revealed
the way a city opens
on a bright landscape
filled with pigeons and the fire of trees
and silver crows also out of sight in the night
and the moon a mouth that one can ignite
and then I wished that you could laugh
and your body bitter
my hands of porcelain on your hips
your breath such a dark–dark pain
a sword at my ear
how often were we here

where only silver shadows stir
only through you I had to deny myself
through you alone I knew I had no harbor
in a burning sea

firewing

when you think of your country
you see
plaited hair and glasses; an old dog smeared with blood;
a horse drowned in the river; a mountain with fire;
a space and two people without teeth in bed;
dark figs against sand; a path, poplars,
house, blue sky, cloud ships;
reeds; a telephone;
you see

when you think of your country
you see that
we must be strong; guts full of craters and flies;
the mountain a butchery without walls;
over the thousand hills of Natal
the fists of warriors like standards;
captives in mud: you see
how mines vomit slaves; the rain
sputtering like sparks against the evening;
among reeds the dwarf's skeleton rots

when you think of your country
all thought is emptied;
when it is clear outside you throw open the windows;
you see stars are arrows in the void;
you hear, quiet as a rumor, do you hear?
we are the people. we are black, but we don't sleep.
we listen in the dark to thieves guzzling in the trees.

we listen to our power that they can never know. we listen
to the heart of our breathing. we hear the sun
shivering in the reeds of night. we wait
until the gluttons fall glutted and rotten from the branches—
a gormandizer will be known by his fruit—
or we'll teach the pigs how to climb trees

the essence of death is jealousy

I will apply well what I learned in the East to reach you
more swiftly. What did I learn in the East? Shut for three
years in a room without light I learnt to walk like the wind.
My eyes are walking sticks feeling for stars because stars are
but stones. I will rise and shake my fists and go home. You
will see me coming from afar and water will stream down
your cheeks so that I may wash the dust from my limbs.
And when we have eaten the fatted calf you will lie on my
breast and ask what did you bring me? Death, I'll say. You
walked all that way to find Death? Yes, but now I know it's
mine. But when you left Death stayed behind; now you're
back it is here once again—I feel him resting in my body
like a shadow in the night. Then I will jump up and smash
all the plates and chuck out the wine and scream: Death, you
betrayed me! Death, you whore!

traveling blind

I spent the night in the shadow of White Mountain
but around the high brows of the peaks
beyond the silver nightcap of eternal snow
I could see the wreaths of light shivering

so huge so untouchable so *white*
so high my understanding will never reach
and through my fingers I tried counting
the prayer beads of stars

to taste your name once again
receive the light drops of your bitter name
murmuring like rain on the tongue
plant your name as an idol in the soil of my dream

a god to bless my onward journey.
for with the calling of your name
with the blood of your name in my mouth
I crawl up ever sparser, ever whiter slopes

jailbird

I'm a night bird on my way to you
with dashes of time
in spouts of darkness
over steppes and savannas
across the meanings of herds of cows
the experiences of nightly seasons
when butterfly freedoms from larval states burst
and the moon grows hot
past memories of the artichoke's
secret stigmata
and the diligent growth of grapefruit farms
thus I come to you;
I'm the night bird traveling to my you
I come from yesterdays and many countries
borne on the passionate trot of the famished beast of prey
in the fanning flight of timid doves
when they spiral away from the sun
sunk in the blue crow's-nest eyes of sailors
woven in the dim locomotive's bitter body
when night whistles through bones
thus I come to you;
with all my maps without roads
for I am the night bird
without gifts or the prettiness of red feathers
but my breath ancient and earth-deep from longing

wind rose

hang out the white sails, beloved
today, not a day later
here and now
we go home

paint blue the boathouse
carefully carefully
take freshwater barrels on board
a palm tree to round off the coasts
oranges my pipes the flowers the bread
and pitch the deck planking
one never knows

what does the compass show?
hang out the white sails, beloved
nail a mountain dove to the highest crosstrees
look, already the wind bulges
warm on the hand

verily today still and forthwith
we set sail
for home:
now all we need is any old sea

Palestine, Israel

war and rumors of war
explosions and chains of fire
devastation dirt roads bullets

slicing through armor and flesh
where the skin is ripped open flowers blurt
or just brazen little eyes

red the flower-blood seeping over leaves
scarlet the tears from black pupils
these are the last days
      for so many soldiers
barefoot through the desert
breathless and with pain

there must be many deaf flies
      in the sand
and white upon white
skeletons
      countdown calendars of war
      and rumors of war

from the radio here the whispering reports of commanders
words that speak of death
statistics temperatures
words foraging without any hunger
the fluttering absent words
from heavenly dwelling places of vultures

words like cartridge cases with the smell of brimstone
words that stink when all sound is burnt away
in Sinai

I write these sentences in a black hotel room
with a small hump of light and rattling window frames
behind the floral curtain

outside a tram trundles across Rembrandtsplein
and autumn's empty leaves whirl back and forth
hopelessly like soldiers made drunk by fear and sorrow
outside the city grumbles
and somewhere in this tomb of concrete and glass
a camel weeps

I write these sentences
even though I walk in the valley of the shadow of death
I shall fear no evil
I shall neither cry nor tremble
nor pick up stones
I shall look with my eyes at the darkness
for you are with me
you walk the road before me
and I feel the flesh under your skin so soft
and high in the fork of your loins it is warm
as in the tongued hollows of the sun
I mount you as if climbing a tree
to shelter like a bird in the hollows of bait
you make my head dizzy with gladness
you strip yourself before my countenance

I hide in you
in your temple-mosque there is asylum
 and linen-clothed tables
  and sweet throat-uttering
   white and fluttering doves . . .
   oh!

—Amsterdam, 1967

the 12th of April, toward evening

farewell:
   of old it would
have been different,
the night of your departure;
we would have had a meal
in a pub on the riverbank
   serenaded by musicians
and comely young women,
the sun would have searched for seating
in branches on the other side, bloodied
like a swan that had flown far
to come and die at water's edge
because swans cannot fly,
   there would have been the rippling flow,
a gargle-fall of clear notes
as the blackbird mocked the evening,
what is passed will not return,
it's the heart of autumn in the body of spring

and we raise high the wineglasses
to bring sparkle to the blood of the swan
and with our sleeves wipe the drops
and crumbs from mustache and lips
to talk against darkness,
suck do-you-remember tales
from the tongue,
hand the ultimate messages back and forth

"do give them my love back home—
embrace my parents, my family, my friends—
what has passed will certainly return,
when the guava trees
are heavy with fruit
and the gardenia by the porch scents the evening
with moon odor in the house of night,
then surely my exile will be lifted . . ."

"don't let the authorities know
how deeply pain eats into me,
it's an ingrown presence
keeping my country raw and alive—
and is it really so mortifying
to watch over crocodiles
here in the North?"

"don't be sad, friend—
tomorrow you'll travel—
    I know
freedom will come to our land
as fertility comes to the earth
from the graves of swans . . ."

outside the stars would have started rustling
and we would hear
how night folds the trees like a wind,
a neighbor's dog barks or coughs
with misty breath a wet flag,
    or we'd have an eternity in the throat,

the night of conversations and silences,
of wine and philosophy and women and resolutions

and with early dawn
I would have startled awake
in a cold hall as gray as ash
    alone,
and have hurried in a trot of short steps
to where the reeds begin,
    the reflection on the water brings tears to my eyes,
far away I see your boat bobbing,
with a wide sleeve I wipe the sun from my eyelashes,
clouds and trees and heaven fall into the stream
and are washed away . . .

but it is long since not of old,
we're not poets,
a layer of dust covers
the silver floor of the departure hall,
    outside in the air
blow streamers of oily smoke and the roar
of fire in metal jet-engines

we have nothing
to say to each other,
you are already bored by the thought
of the long sit ahead,
    I worry
about heavy traffic
back to the gray city,
    the heart is gray

you drink a lemonade, I a beer:
"give my love to,
you know, everyone"

"perhaps we'll meet again,
I also just don't know"

words are swallowed,
ingested, have fallen from memory,
    flights are announced
like an impersonal wind from far away

you are returning to your country,
it is not my country—
you are returning to your country,
it is no longer my country

the flame at the mouth

The day suicide occurs to me I will have to borrow an
evening suit somewhere so as to be fittingly dressed for the
occasion. I will wear a dress shirt with lace stitched to the
front, and a bow tie—one of those you have to tie yourself,
not the clip-on kind. My shoes will be black, patent leather
and polished, and my socks light yellow. I will have had my
hair cut for the first time in years, and spattered my whiskers
with eau de toilette. I will dip in mint water one of those
little wooden spoons that you find in ice cream cups, before
putting it in my mouth, on the tongue: it keeps the breath
fresh and prevents the tongue from being swallowed. Ah, but
it will be such a splendid event!

With shoes still creaking nearly imperceptibly I'll climb
on a chair and arrange a velvet bell-cord around my neck.
Then I will shut my eyes for the last time, to see the hills in
the darkness, and say: "The dogs hunt for John through the
freshly ploughed tomato fields!" and launch myself from the
chair into space. I hope I will be smiling despite the mint-
flavored spoon in the mouth.

After a while the steward will make his call, carrying a tray.
He will ask, "Did you ring, sir?" and then his thoughts will
lose themselves and his eyes will have a far-off look, and sunk
in dreams he will spill the glass of liquor over my still slightly
quivering socks and shoes. It will be a vodka and tomato
juice, a Bloody Mary, so that it will seem as if I had waded in
blood. For many years now I have been walking ankle-deep
in viscous, lurid blood.

The Undanced Dance
(Poems from Prison, 1975–1982)

two scandaroons upsky flash the first
last orange sunswords—
thus to call upon the gods
outside time and time at the dead bird ritual of birth
to create everything out there inside for one slash:
it is good to comb the watch-arms over soft ciphers
as well while alive still to die

—Gonefi Shing

Chopin's fingers

to float to the surface from night's pond,
debris, putrid mirror, the noose of darkness
still narrowing the neck, the tune of nocturnal colors
that purified is now just water,
and try hiding in the light—mouthing
the ballad of absence in a long-forgotten measure—
I wake up with the wet taste of ivory and rook

knowledge of pain and consciousness of death—
the private careening, vacillation and demise of the impulse
within monotonous walls of the cell, minute red cough
                              on the meager grass—
but also the municipal
abdication: the light-exploding leveling
when systems fold, the communal inner space
a public hole without circumference

and knowing that this knowledge is blind, instinctive
stench from birth,
and the realization, never realized, that this pure vision
of blinding knowledge—
when with neither rhyme nor reason the shaft of knowing
nibbles around ancient edges of the void—
is an amulet, keening protection against death

thus alone do you dare to dance, aware of the laws
of captivity—never to trust, that betrayal will be
for a slice of bread, a vague promise of parole
or the small preferment to pimp—and to rely,

ensnared, on the loyalty of other cells,
bodies stuffed with dying, mutations of self;
to save the gray moth under the shower

why is there singing in the slave quarters?
all dying is double, multiplied stains
in the shards—but imagination's plicae
wear away and the unthinkable finds its shape:
in a glass cage I see you, I see us each
an individual wilting—sun moths—ah, to live
in this absurd world if only momentarily
with the earnestness of a flower—

to hold on to your image as a screening
from death's
deeper insight, my mask,
my mate,
my amulet,
my murmurous healing of the flame,
my minuscule moment of rook and ivory

destination

to the sea we cannot go back
the sea has grown old
with white wrinkles and foam around the lips

we cannot return to the desert
there's violence behind the dunes
ant fortresses on their way to war
in pale valleys the jackals trot through light nights
each within the cool zareba of his shadow steps

all borders are now fronts and fire lines
we are well up shit creek

here we shall dawdle
where the suburbs have been leveled
and soiled grave diggers live in cellars
transparent as if of the present
self-contained like faucets
deaf to their own dripping
the blind things devouring corpses
with nothing to show
except second-mouth false teeth

here the hands of sextons
are shivering with wrinkles and the foam
from dark corpses they had to wash
perfuming bridegrooms for the bridal bed

here we tumble
implosively
to new interior boundaries

the dream

I dreamed:
I'm in a prison of white walls
where nobody knows me where voices
go absent in corridors where lights sough
my skull wheezes
I saw myself:
squat to shit in a bucket flies
come with the summer nights
the lights sigh white flames
I saw my name:
shift down the lists with nobody
to read remember
ever more dimly through annual
anal rings
curved into the white of the jail

I awoke:
when the judas-eye looked astart at me

December

following rhythm and road of a poem by Gary Snyder

Six a.m., jingle
    of night commander
    speeding closer; keys crack
    down the corridor
out there birds arbor, tinkling
tiny bells; in the minute
meshed yard pansies unfold
like moths flagging down the day;
stretch the pallet with bedding on bunk;
in the Section bath and shave.
    N, the cleaner, silent, pimpled
    white prison feet,
    brings the porridge, "coffee," bread
    (who's trying to sell me short?)

Voice of Section Chief: Jump to it!
Jump to it! Clean up! Move arse!
Inspection. Cement floor shimmering
a shaven face.

Out for exercise round
    and round the sightless pansies.
    Boer's cap-badge, whiskers, gleam.
    Cut the pocketchief lawn short
    and scour slop bucket white:
    wind weeping in some wireless tree.

Ten-thirty, lunch: boiled mealies,
beets, maybe meat. Dixies out!
Rinse and wedge spoon in door.
Eleven o'clock the cell's locked:
      midday snooze
   draw deep at the fag
  and listen to the Philistines rag.

Two o'clock, shining the floor
once more, Brasso on copper; Ghostkeeper's
   chill eye ringed by the judas;
   try making contact with connection.
  Cell ransacked—someone
  must have quacked.
  Stretch the pallet with bedding on bunk.

Three-thirty, graze: soup, "coffee,"
   yellow eye of butter
   framed by bread.
   Dixies out! Buck up!
Rinse off and spoon in door,
both shoes lined up
without feet on corridor floor.
   Four o'clock the cell is locked:
   Get up! Stand to!
   Jailbird countdown all motherfuckers you!

Lights on. Dusk
might be falling outside like prayer. Manna.
Listen how being locked up grinds.
            Talk to self.

Condemned sing. Outside, birds
mirror the tilted
tiny bell sounds; in the tight
meshed yard pansies fold together
like flags turned to moths in the night.

Eight o'clock, slumbertime, lights out
      and fire of yearning.
Limelight and torch-blur on catwalk,
rifle butts thud.
      Heart burns: sweet
      smoke in nostrils,
      thoughts scuffle:
a *mugu* sobs and bleats in the bush of sleep.

Zazen. Steel and concrete folds
where stars quiver;
      the guard's beat is god
      in the head—
      but stillness in the crop
      breath's penitential exercise.

Sit till midnight. Silently
      invoke this day's negative.
      Bow deep to the wall

and stretch the pallet out on bunk.
Stiff under sheets:
white.

     Jingle
of night commander
speeding closer

the commitment

I suspect
but I won't bet my life on it
that there's a country
behind the fast walls of this labyrinth

I dream
I can't say why
of a space as spacious as a dream
and light like tea stains on the bridal gown

and hillocks not unlike freshly cudgeled brains
still smoking and quivering in the morning
of mountains with the color of heavenly
blazes aged to ashes
the teeth of the dragon snow-bleached by the sun
and that all this will inexplicably flare up in the night

that there's a disquieting sea
writing shorelines where whales will come calving
a white shakiness
and fertile zones for the mango and the pear
also the desert
for small mammals to nibble at the wind
and at times a city like a blade oh so proud
with a rust-eaten grip in the withered hand

that the ribbon around the temples must rot away
and thoughts run free—

for this I don't give a poet's damn
for I am God
an impregnable keep

but something makes me wonder
I don't know what
about trains ripping a shimmering spear
and tracks in the vastness
and lorries and fleapits and pain
and cedar trees and confusion and landing strips
and vineyards and poverty
and sometimes the language rings a familiar bell
as if I could remember myself out of this predicament

then I dig down deeper into obscurity
and think
oh if only I could
what would happen
were I to climb up the walls
to chant from the parapet
"Good morning, Sout' Efrica, I love thee!"

sweet and somber

sweet and somber breath streamed all night through my
    window,
and the silver bracken of the moon—and other matter
throbbed in space—tatters, snapshots, flitting memories,
filaments of what we never could gather furnished the
    dream—
surgery cluttered with bloody washbowls and chrome
where from the gorgeous circles of our love Stephan Jerome
was born—but you and that red squirming bird
were absent, gone—locked behind my eyes I have a tree
heavy with footsteps and rags binding my life to me—
other rooms, bird vocals, memory people, old folk dried by
    life
kissing the offspring, your beauty like evergreen leaves—
in the dead ear of the telephone I hear our never-born child
sing—the sweet and the somber still vibrate through the
    string
from a belly now big with age—and the silver tresses of the
    moon

poem on toilet paper

nights everything is possible
this red labyrinth that I inhabit
        like a rat
its echoing passages and frowns of steel barriers
   fade away
       only floodlights and solitary warders
ring the darkness in rising towers
   the jail becomes a monastery

from the bunk I take the pillow
and roll it tight
   this is my *zafu*
to the wall inside the sacred space
       I make *sampai*
deep in the ear coils the hollow pain
of the gonged wooden fish
and I cross my legs and breathe
and I see nothing
and nothing is seen
thus to turn back to reality

through walls the *mayas* break
spouting desires
       flames in the crotch
   burning images of the world
how deep will this land live on within me?
that the heart may never be blunted or blurred!

till the corpse is thrown on the town square
where curs flash their sweet fangs
and only turds paint the fields—
kill! kill that which has not lived!

it also pales
    the inner quad
becomes a haven for night birds
the moon has grown feathers
outside a tree stretches its roots
    to peer in
    and look upon darkness
where all is honed
    to a mountain of time endlessly unearthed

which recedes in time
    the wound closes up again
in this place I do *kin hin*
and listen to the breath that comes and goes
until it will stop coming
                    to go

when light bleeds
I *gassho* to the wall
I sit in sun's snow
    and leave my chopped-off arm
        on the writing book
            a flower to the silence

all around is jail
the way has no end
but what does it matter?

—*Pretoria Maximum Security*

the wise fool and *ars poetica*

thus he decided to go forth
deeper into the region of vowels and consonants
where pure sounds sprout (though also other thrusts
and clever lips cutting short the very breath:
mouse-birds among the figs), to areas
where sense and nonsense flourish, where strophes
climb in odd places and strange and bitter fruit may
    happen—
or so he was told, and mused:
the oppressed goes out in the early morning
to look for solutions, or failing all
an ersatz for the bloated fidgetiness; the fool
folds his hands and consumes his own flesh

it was quiet there (unpolluted by orb or orifice),
a thrumming silence, a calm redolent of smack
and suck, of oh and ay; he was at sea,
and deprived of the stick-and-track of needle and map
his eyes slithered over the boned black expanse,
scouting for vegetation or visitation or just a flash
that might point the way to the well of inspiration,
even if needs be (who was *he* to be bullfrogged
with pride?), a ladle of well-chewed castaway victuals:
for a live dog is better than a dead lion

vanity, all vanity; all about him the barren words
were as sand upon sand; he scanned his self
in the sand and moaned (thus it is written:

the offended will spit and shriek against the wind,
but the lips of the fool will devour him
and darken the nest egg to naught):
"Fathead, may you swallow an umbrella
and may it open in your bowels ..."
or "may you lose all your teeth except one
and that one be sharpening the ache ..."
or: "may flies settle shuddering colonies
in the clefts of your armpits and the shuttle of your
    thighs ..."

when at last there was a lunar paleness
and he as spent as time and tide, he went
to lay down arms and bones in the desert
(beyond horizons the neon verdict of nightclubs);
and tumbled into sleep: look, laid out he was
in a striped *djellaba* with his lute as mute as the flower,
and a dog-tamed lion alive with the moon's silvery mane
came to sniff his breath and eavesdrop at his ear ...

  so that now we'll never know
  whether the mangy meat-eater
  mustered sufficient curiosity or teeth
  to make an end
  to this poem

there is life

there are christs spiked against trees
prophets in the wilderness seized with fits
worshippers whose eyes bud under the sun
buddhas on one side conversing with figs

there is life greening in the clouds
while dolphins shred through loops of waves
the seagull's swerving gut-lean shriek
and barefooted scragginess along mountain flanks

behind magnifying sky the crater's firespeech
inclines of snow like silences shift
when heaven cracks open hairline wide
and spills black legends the swallow the dove

there are bones that bind the earth
delight that breaks through what's time-bound
and blunderer droll notion that I may be
I'll still grow rich on daylight's beam

scales flared the whole night through
I might once have been a prisoner too
but here the heart's pulsing contract is spelled:
a hundred years from now we will all be bare

freezing point

Legs wide he stands, the sun,
his chill dripping a flickering ice-cone,
a hairy flame at the core of coldness. A shivering sound
become stone. Legs wide he stands, back arched
against the livid circling heavens, and allows the mirror
to be seen: wherein no image glitters
nor anything but blank intensity.

On the bathroom wall a sheet of steel
holds the liquid outlines of inmates made to shave
without ever seeing clear enough to slit their own throats:
the jugular pulses subterranean. In the breast I feel apples
of decay and in my wrists the racing trains.
Now—after how many months of solitary confinement?—
a true mirror suddenly is brought into my cell, a watching
pool of water, but below the frozen surface
a stool pigeon beckons, a wrinkled blanched ape
most probably from China, gesticulating immoderately
and creasing my mouth in an inane grimace
when he catches my eye. Layer upon layer, grin over smirk
and the grayness of ash. His mouth is the bloody obscurity
of the apple's interior, livid fungus is flecked about his eyes.
A thing has come to grow in the brightness: and I'm no
      longer alone.
I shall have to count my words.

How did this occur? Winter like apples,
gray moldering in the earth. And the wind

crumpling ash, rags, newspaperwords, cadavers of dogs,
bullet cartridges, the open arteries of the roads:
the corpses, guts thick with blowflies in cupped hands.
And above the graphic of smoke swerve steel-eyed
    helicopters.

Higher still, a periscope rising out of the blue, the splinter ice.

for the singers

for the singers
you singing from dusky holes
as bees must do in a field with no flowers
you lamenting consolation where there's no relief
calling out to a Savior for recourse and no rescue
can ever save you
singing as if your lives depended on it

the singers; for you
who smell the gathering obscurity
like cattle at the slaughtering places
the day shriveling night after night
hour by hour each song is bent back
and threaded in the rope,
can any voice go tell it on the mountain?

you will not see the veldt with its smells
the smoke above steel cities of our terrible land
not the birds thumb-tumbling from the clouds
nor tiny insects building huts in the loam
neither flash of motorcar nor happiness of birth
not the horse's gallop or sun's fury and extravagance
nor the young women

only the rope will know you
and for now too the song
the heart, the heart a one-life stand

but in the singing is twined the endlessness
of dying—with melancholy
praise the Lord God or the Prophet
who giveth peace when night lies
on its dark cutting edge
abidance from the Buddha behind joss sticks
with his swollen apple-eyes of compassion—
what for? all over man
is death and dust
and only in others he reverberates

could I do so I'd have you as guests
where waves are beached
gravitated by the solidity of shells
where people feast at silver linen tables
and why not the Scala and the Crazy Horse Saloon
the flatlands around Beograd
seabird islands surging close by Bergen
where there's dancing and hooting where winds
evoke chasms among the ridged peaks . . .

what's tomorrow?
West? a paradise with lovely holiday chalets?
—angels lay no eggs—
a never-ending road with butterflies? the chilly
murmuring of pismire and worm
when everything becomes insignificant, to be destroyed?
a void in the cell?
but the voices remain

but everywhere man is dust and death and his groaning
   is as nothing
the one cleaves to the other and strings him up
the hands of the one claw open the other's gorge
thus the law sings, such is man, so the darkness rings
the outer and the inner
and life doesn't die
everywhere man lives on in the people

for you, singing from the dark
of your ultimate daybreak—take, eat—
let your chant be like the breast
of the bird steeped in honey

and I shall retain the sweetness
for as long as my tongue may tremble
hanging in the mouth of bittersweet life

— *"Beverley Hills," 9/19/75*

the conquerors

because we refused to see them as people
all that was inside us wasted away
and we find no more tears to bemoan our dying
    because we wanted nothing but hatred and fear
we ignored their uprising clamoring for humane laws
and hoarsely tried to find ways out but all too late
the flower's in the fire

not a soul could care for our solutions

we are past all cluck–cluck comprehension
we are of some other dimension
we the children of Cain

    because we came before God with covetous pleading
God hollowed our words and in vain
we now call out from closet and garden upon porch
in the enclosures that we are the chosen ones

not a soul could be bothered by our hatred and our fear

the fruit rots on the tree, the stalks
silt up on the land / oil and salt grow scarce
the laborer's hand slips from the plough
to grasp for weapons / they will be lifted against us
for we are already out of time / targets of dislocation
signs of annihilation / which will fade with time's
    consummation

    because we wished to pour lavishly of that blood
it grew heavy and weighed past the strength of our hands
these hands which into the sods we pitch
clouds big with voices

not a soul to weep over our gifts and our death

what remains are coat, empty farmstead, shaft of mine
what cleaves to the root of being clots this sudden pain
of a dispossessed solitary path through the white bull's-eye

for François Villon

there are things one never forgets, oh dissemblers—
cat's paws of darkness over closed eyelids
the brief clear gaping of the bullet's cough
car headlamps slitting the night to ribbons
painted white masks of the buffoon and the whore
the hangman's laughter like a dose of strychnine
the flesh-colored flame
                         that cannot scorch the satin purse
black rooks on red haystacks
a dwarf with a whistle on the elephant's back
the tower filled years since with whispering fire
the green swollen booming of the sea
the long broken downhill shuffle of old age
braking till it's worn to the knees—
these, the inalienable souvenirs
the heart's tiny mirrors lugged the length of the journey

we all walk that road
of life on its way to death—
murderers, burglars, drug addicts and firebugs
thugs, embezzlers, rapists
and fellow terrorists—
you like me tattooed in lineament and skin
single in our destiny—
till we climb through the gap
into the kitchen pantry
and the earth munches us to the bone
"finished; dispatched; cracked; home"

go well, friends, by the light of the body
go well, marked by what's never forgotten
to the final prison where all memory goes dark
hamba kahle!

memory two

he will remember—
broken dawn mornings, the city robed in gray
and the distant droning for no apparent reason—
triple of hooves, a tump, a flood—
the relaxed warm spine in the bed,
steaming bowl of tea and hand-pale bread
and then, with rain flicking the frozen glass face,
on a pushbike through the city's misty canyons
past trees all bloated and leaking and glittering
with fog, to the *dojo*
(only later the sun will bark like a gardened dog),
the cool black folds of breath
imploding silence,
                              and soon, from the belly's depth—
Maka Hanya Haramita Shingyo:

he will remember—
rough worker's garb of bottle brothers in the bistro,
salutations, clickety-clack of words rubbing import,
and knives, dark blush on white napkin of light
through a wineglass, red steak, salad green,
the gentle contact with comradely eyes
and up! to work!
smell of turpentine and fresh linen canvas

he will remember—
the glow of flames in eyes darkly dreamt
of the woman curled before the gated fire,
journeys paced in days along mountain coils

so white the eye feels skinned, and down
among rice paddies, through gold-flecked Siena dusks,
he'll remember the woman searching for cockles
by the rim of blue waters
edging a desert where a wind
huffs soundlessly, and is peeled black

he will remember—
the mad moon, an embered hand
from the ocean making feathered papillae
of the silvered palm trees, with shadows
clotting as fancy takes them, coating,
carrying forests, to croak

he will remember
the sun for one timeless beat
fluttering a blood-stained bird in his fingers
to soar like a wall then way beyond
any sconce or dungeon's narrow reach:

gya tei gya tei hara-so gya tei
bo-ji so wa-ka

Hanya Shingyooo . . .

transit

this land is scored brown by winter
melancholy comes upon it with each evening's fall
when the sky cracks a ripe dove's egg
the veld notched and folded over with shadows
gnawed brown by the locust folk
singeing black tracks toward moisture or grass
and brown before that with primeval caresses
it's an indifferent land

the smoke of winter folded over the earth
in the brown twilight nestling birds chitter
or bud on telephone wires
the sod pungent with winter smoke
made sweet by subterranean heat

in a convoy we journeyed southward
no one could hear the clacking of our shackles
the vehicles on the highway, shiny-eyed owls
guzzling all travelers down tooth and flail
and only later spewing up the hair and the nails
we are indigestible! indivisible! free!
now walleyed at the peek of the pickup van window
I see moon and stars swelling like tears
outside the sweep of time's orbit

this land is all the seasons of the night
now and then we rattled through dead country towns
where no one could hear the clocking of our shackles
through empty streets flared by lines of shop windows

with glassbound mannequins coldly mumming the latest
  styles
    and softly walk-softly a black petrol jockey
hooded in gray balaclava and grayer greatcoat
an enduring ghost watching all things come and go

in the small hours a frostfall of stars
perhaps there were jackals in the hills
but by the first shimmer of morning
the world was too cold for kapok
and when we had to fill up with fuel
it was on an island in a sea of visions
of naked bush and gray land sea-deserted
a million years ago
       early laborers
were on the way from nowhere to work
trudging all behind their cold footsteps
under the live foam of the clouds
and could not hear the clicking of our shackles

deeper south the mountain chains were
white mirrored heliographs peaking above the green ambush
and regimentation of vineyards in the lowlands
humble indentations of the landsman's investiture
glassy slit veins of water waiting for the spring

again evening came bruising through
      only one further phase of winter's invention
each journey has its time-bound reach and intention
just as the verse on the line must know the point of its
  turning

and above the new prison the smoky moon was burning
a pale ship intact on frozen black sand
in the east a crackling ice palace lay stranded

through the hatches sweet swollen odor of night flowers
magnolia and sea mixing in bruised evening delight
the clickclackclocked throats of the toads
the inquisitive patter and twitter of peewits
and with growing light the seagull's gray commentary
upon the sfumato signature of this seaboard
lifting mists against the mountains' solid obscurity

like silver thoughts the clouds will roll open
how magnificent the earth below!

—*8/10–11/1977*

mountain prison
to the memory of Marius Schoon

the mountain, so I imagine, fort where primeval shadows
can lie blackened from the light,
the mountain is full of herbs and old smells

nights when from the stronghold darkness comes,
the sweet breath of healing plants bruised
by an unsuspecting buck's hoof
or simply the unfolding of extinct flowers,
the temple-making, the hallowing wide

nights I have to think of you, exiled one,
that you cannot inhale this darkened joy,
can no longer be cured by deep sadness
and perhaps will have to choke on foreign soil

but then I think further: imagination
and memory shape one sweet mountain,
with clods in the mouth we are both
but gray recumbent possession

your tracks now cross over another beach
yet we each cherish the yearning for one
mountain-high fire
to purify obscurity and bring us to silence

mountain of alliance between you and me,
mountain of ecstasy,
mountain of appeasement,
bittersweet mount of irreality

—*Pollsmoor*

sanctuary

from the very start it was destined to be thus
that you would cast us aside
first with jeers and gossip talk
blunt clasp-knives laying bludgeons bare
then with mockery and blatant blacking of names
as we moved further out from the circle of joviality
the supple latticework of shadows
under fig trees the dreams of mouse birds,
I with my granddad a brittle bone bundle on the back
and my father a-stumbling close at hand,
away from ancient orchards the rippling tranquility
                              of ringwalls
tomato fields with sprinkled irrigation
silverfish landscapes below speeding cloud—

there were insects in your beards
a slipperiness about the supple pips of your eyes
and weak spittle-threads twined red around your tongues
but your smothered laughter and jests were worse than
    dog-barks
you high priests of bigotry—

the farther you chased us the more impudent you became
regressing mindlessly to brutal archetypal ways
rooting communally for a psychic amnesia
under mud lies buried the god idea of pigs—

when night shrank you drove us along other roads,
I with my granddad huffing like heavy wings on my hump

and my father a mumbling closer at hand,
till we ran for sanctuary in the deer park
and then in barbarous bloodlust you broke the zoo gates
                              open too—

and under rents in the stillness
black the inlay the ribbing of uproar and rot
we who were dissenters were now the hunted prey
blundering through hedges
across whisper-filled savannas trying to break free
                              to a new day
among zebras whose lines had flowed away
and buffaloes with hides gnawed bright by lice
old age is a parasite—

and on our trail you came snickering degenerate laughter
by the light of battle-axes and a sputtering of flares
your dim heads with bruise-marked features
mouths slackened into idiotic leers
and you no longer had the knowledge of who you were
no laws linking freedom to accountability
no conscience fielded by boundaries of reference—
except that we must be crushed one and all

father

and you came forth from the old patriarch's loins,
from a clan of hard and bitter inlanders:
drifters who trekked a dusty heaven in their quest
for the subterranean water star, for a course, a pass,
for the survival of threshing floor and haystacks;
the interior sea with gray crests, with brown crests,
the donkey cart a caravel setting sail; diehards
whose blood even the ants could not disperse,
rebels, nomads
through the wilderness they named life;
wheat one year and khaki-weed when the seasons turn;
from fatling and kitchen garden to goatherd and taskwork,
from farmstead to squatter's shack; leggings and *velskoene*,
turtle doves and locusts, jackals and shadow-curs;
   iguanas he strung up in the kloofs at full moon;
he had no book-learning but decency to spare and share
and his heart was a bible;
in his somber eyes he could hold the mountains,
   look for the hiding holes of the morning star,
his hands giant shells filled with the reverberations of the
   earth:

and he died and was gathered in among his fathers,
he died and climbed into the ground
to sit mumbling among the quartz chips and clods of clay
where bushy-haired roots fiercely track the water down
   and rock crystallizes color layer upon layer,
he died with the first dew and clambered into the trees,

the sun a light mantle on his shoulders,
his hair alive with cawing crows:

love one another his teeth signal in the wind,
the flesh passes, peeling away blue,
the shells grow luminous
(at times, I know, I am the pod
in which his restless bones knock and nod):

and you,
have you truly harnessed that sleepless blood?
I remember you out on the veranda, your dark eyes
fixing the small foxes in the vineyard
and the shadows rising from the hills,
your hands salty and damp, your boots
staking out their claim, limber and brown
you scatter rubies across the grass, crackle of glass;
I see you walking tall under the fruit trees
conversing with twilight configurations, how few your words;
after supper you lay your evening prayers like peasant bread
   on a linen tablecloth;
you sit forked upon your steed to scout over the horizon
         for obstacles to come;
you hunker on the mountaintop with your ruminations
         down below in the sweet valleys,
and you summon the feathered ones, fiscal shrike, sparrow,
         wagtail, and swallow;
you wait on the high dune caressing with knitted brow the
   green water,
the white horses, the godsend:

and now you are old and just a breath short of eternity,
you will live on forever
in this clan of hard and bitter inlanders,
travelers hunched round campfires in the nocturnal skies,
the great place of outspanning,
till first light rises from the earth and the erring is resumed:

now you are old and darkened and I have your bones
            your deep blood
and the soughing of your breast
oh father, bless me before you go

mother

and you were born out of the old gentleman's loins,
he of the upright torso waistcoated and watch-chained,
the town-going fedora and glasses swimming with soft eyes;
among farmer folk who kept an ample but penniless
    homestead
where the first mountains encyst their solitude,
the Sandveld, dune world (visions of white harvest fields
with cool blue-gums tokening rest), in the company of them
who burr their consonants because they love one another
and the grace of the sea: Struisbaai, Stilbaai, Spoelbaai,
    Dansbaai,
where strange treasures wash ashore: kists of marbles, copper
bedsteads, books, jars of balm, dead predicants, crosses,
    sextants
and curvaceously carved bowsprit nymphs from another
    hemisphere;
the sea of grace
where you will never know whether waves have eyes of
    laughter
or tears, and each rainbow drags its veil thick with rain:
(soothsayer, say, which is more blue: the mountain sky,
sea-shimmer, or my grandfather's speck-bespectacled eye?)

impoverished, his house? no, even though he humbly lay
    down roads
of pebbles and sand for the Divisional Council,
    his house was a haven melodious with names:
Sebastiaan, Rachel, Johannes, Bettie, Schalk, Martha, Anna,

Bert and Susanna and right on till daybreak; there were the
    quadrille
and the polka, squeezebox and mandolin, music for Africa;
on their charitable erf they cultivated their own bulrush
and broom bush, sorrel and marigold and heather and
    laughter;
from the sea's recesses came *alikruikels, perlemoen, harders,*
    kabeljou;
trees were heavy with sun; in the larder *konfyts* and meats and
    flour,
in the kitchen pancakes and honey
from those bee-filled graves, so the blossoms grew;
and nights when the moon rode down every cloud,
and other nights when stillness rolled from horizon to
    horizon,
the Southern Cross smoking in its cradle, Orion, Rigel,
    Betelgeuse,
Procyon, Aldebaran, Sirius, Eridanus, Antares, Canopus,
    Arcturus,
Eastern Cross, Centaurus the clod of gold
and other star branches acrackle and asmolder . . .

and he died and was gathered in among his kin,
he died like glass eyes toppling from the bedside table,
he died and went to bloom a few fathoms deep,
blossoming twigs massed with galaxies, graves topped with
    sweetness:

                    then you,
I grew up under your skirts;
when I think of you I see shy cheeks and plaits,

an apron full of flowers and a green sun hat:
I never know if you're laughing or crying

   ("oh rubbish!" you snort),
and I smell the warm sea-vulnerable earth
and cinnamon and cloves and flowers: snapdragons,
   kalkoentjies,
larkspurs, roses, sword lilies, *perdeklou*, pansies, zinnias,
magnolias, *uiltjies,* frangipanis, *bobbejaantjies*, gardenias,
poinsettias, pig's ears: your tongue gives pollen and petals
and bees, yes, you speak flowers, you heal what hurts,
you bind the rain in a spell of light;
I hear you hum at the harmonium
and see you turn the shadows blue; the sea breeze nestles
in your hair, a small ruby flickers on your finger;
for you the fullness is created at the backdoor
and all the world throbs out front
always brimming with delight: ah, life swift as the flick
of a wrist and your hands are never still; butterflies of love
hover above your head:

and now you are old, saturated with living and young forever,
like a fruit tree in the soil:

I bear your bones your careening blood
and the sing-song sounds of your throat
oh mother, bless me before you go

the wake

when my mother was dying
I had to flay my way through the seething current
to reach the bedstead where they had laid her out
in the yard: shimmering yellow,
the sun stroked the arcadian scene
playing up the choir of ancient faces of extinct
uncles and forefathers sitting peacefully
sucking pipes to warble smoke,

strong and chipper she was under the white sheet
her eyes luminous and somewhat surprised without the
    glasses
her plumpish arms distributing with decisive gestures
the ultimate advice and blessings
(only the tired gray bun had already come undone),
visions of everything going swimmingly and she
at rest now with Matthew and Mark to her left
and right the two old geezers were by Jove standing to,

and she kept on beckoning me by name
and could not recognize me,

but I had to head back lest the authorities
get wind of my evasion into the water's
quickening whirl I sank
(was this to be the great drowning?)
to wash up chatter-teeth lower down between banks
somewhere past farmlands where mud-spattered

granaries splinter the heavens where haystacks
rot and turnips are gorged down by turf,

and straining at their leashes I heard the stinking dogs
throat-clogged with the yelping fury of the hunt

as of wings

Dearly beloved, I'm sending you a laughing dove
for no one will shoot a red message.
I throw my laughing dove high above
and I know all the hunters will think it's the sun.
Look, my dove rises and my dove goes down
and where it flies the oceans glitter
and trees become green
and it paints my tidings so red on your skin

For my love travels with you,
my love must stay an angel at your side
like wings, white like the angel.
You must go on knowing my love
the way you have wings
with which you cannot fly

Isis

when your hand caresses me once more
do it carefinger carefully
remember I am no longer whole
pieces are gone patches scorched
with the years, the other's share
scabbed over, sore, the envelope
is rough and dully shrunken to torso
with limbs and the chopped logic
of nerve motives

dim like ice
with acerbity of smoke in fiber and membrane
through pucker and crack deceased
up to the deadened epidermis

for too long have I forgotten
the deft tips of fondling
the flower fingering of dalliance
woven in a carpet of arabesques

perhaps you should steal a wing somewhere

we should go plundering
a crumbled totality
frayed to the ultimate strophe
we must venture over the hard rind
of frozen water behind
the mirror dolphins trace a playful parabola
somewhere profoundly tip and tuck

and meanwhile so dark
how everything in the dark dips and ducks
half a life prawn plankton krill
predacious fish seal eel
also the rotten carcasses
of sunken discovery barks

clean it must be to plunge through a flaw
in the white-word-floe skin
plumbing deeper down into the healing
oblivion, *whole then*
again when your hand writes me over

jantra

many a year the mountain's not been as green
such a proud sparkling gem
as in this early panoply of dying;
it is the passage to segregation—
autumn squandered its riches in burnt hues
and the force of renewal slumbers
lifelessly curled on Sesha's coils—
and yet each day is pure and still
so that the most shell-sheltered particularity
with a brightness bringing to mind life
stands clear from full to overflowing
crest unto the furthermost chime
under sun's cicatrix

with peaks ever more fair under mourning snow
my beloved, along the mountain passes we'll go
up to the hips in white oblivion
and from the coldest and sharpest-toothed summit
hand in hand (since together we sprout wings)
wu wei wu wei fearlessly plunge
a fall endlessly away to the fertile god-patched valley
now such a long greening shout ago

—*Vesak, 1981*

your letter

your letter is larger and lighter
than the thought of a flower when the dream
is a garden—
          as your letter opens
there's an unfolding of sky, word from outside,
wide spaces

I slept in green pastures,
I lay on the cusp of the valley of the shadow of death
during the last watch of the night
listening to those condemned to die
being led through tunnels in the earth,
          how they sing
with the breath at their lips
as residents at the point of leaving
a city in flames, how they sing,
their breaths like shackles,
          how they sing—
they who are about to jump from light into darkness,
they who will be posted to no destination—
terror fills me at the desecration

the table before me in the presence of my enemies
is bare, I have ash on my head,
my cup is empty

and I fled to your letter to read
of the orange tree decked out in white blossoms
opening with the sun,

I could smell it on the balcony—
　　　　I can smell you
lovelier and lighter than the thought of a flower
in this dismal night

I will be suspended from the sky of your words—
grant that I may dwell in your letter
all the days of my life

envoi
your letter is wonderful, larger and lighter
than the thought of a flower when the dream
is the earth of a garden—
　　　　　　as your letter opens
there's an unfolding of sky, word from outside,
memory

the riding song of the bridegroom

when it's *moussem* again in Imilchil
and the Imazighen come down
from black frowns and folds of the Atlas mountains
to barter sheep for salt and seed
I will load my donkey with tent ropes and mats
twist paradise dreams in the lengths of my head cloth
with a white tongue in the neck
to show you how eager I am
for love
and legs astride astride legs ride through the gorge

when it's *moussem* again in Imilchil
where the many tents cower like great seagulls spreading
wide their wings around the sweet mausoleum of
                              Sidi Mohammad el Merheni
panting for a breeze from the mountain heights
I'll come looking for you
amid the wreathing bee-bodies of marketers

look for your black eyes your veiled voice the whispering
flow of your silhouette
I want to read the gimp of the lining of your hand
please let me buy you your wedding gown

my mountain gimmer my desert fruit
when it's *moussem* again in Imilchil
I'll know you from the kohl around your eyes the carmine

on your cheeks the cape of woven color over the bride-
    white robe
and around your throat the clouds of happiness and my good
    fortune
in silver and amber and clouded glass
for you have taken hold of my liver

the marabout's honey is a thesis in dust
you will rub a handful over your white-seamed breasts
to exorcise winter's pale nights with summer
and the pollen of bees—
I will pay the *qadi* my bride-price
and free of bygones and state and tribe
let my dust lie down intimately with yours

tonight we'll roast the *mechouï* over embers of the vine
and nibble at the fat sheep's white eye with our teeth
the juicy udder and the mountain oysters
tonight we roust hump-backed on the ululating flute's wail
around flames licking closer and clearer than the stars

and when the earth turns . . .
come return with me to my eternal bed of snow
behind white fortress walls on the roof of the day
where the fig tree mutters its royal shaded recitations
and pomegranates are golden cheek-mirrors on the slopes
come to where the heart of the well figures deep black water
so you may hoodwink me with the rock-rocking of seasons
and teach me how blossoms flower the whole year through

because you took possession of my liver—

be the staypole of my tent my mountain fruit my desert
  gimmer
let me strip the bridal finery from your tattooed sweetroot
  bush
and legs astraddle without saddle ride to heaven through the
  cleft

metabolic

when I climb on the chair
to wipe the southeaster's golden dust
from the high windowsill
I see beyond the tungsten bars
for the fraction of an opening
two swallows dallying against the evening sky
by turns catching the shine of a dying earth
to flutter like leaf-barks cut loose
from the eternal celestial-blue blue gum tree
free, free,
freely slipping and stitching from fire to dream;
and there's life in the metabolism between eye and flight
around the arc of revolution silenced in smoke
my friend, my sister, my wife—
for every hour from the oldest sign on
has been a rite of give and take

"to live is to burn"
Andrei Voznesensky

all is luminous and all is still: to live is to be
digested like this summer day of loveliness; ever
and again to praise the globe rocking by, the sultry leafage
of thickets, water-slips, stone lips, the feathered ones'
    heart-chips
changed to chain eyes linking silence to silence; how totally
    rich
the mountain, naked, sun-caked—only one plume whitening
the wind which soon must bulge with slender organ sounds
and streamers; and it is done, spiraling the cycle of seasons
has heaved old wrinkles like worms from the womb—
but look, we are each the coachman of oblivion, rigor mortis
with bleached hands at death cart's reins. prayer by prayer
our way is cocked, cool, a skeleton chaliced in day-dress of
    flesh . . .

burn, burn with me love—to hell with decay!
to live is to be alive, while alive to die anyway

liberation

here I am this first day already shimmering bright
among angel choirs: afar the feathered folk sing psalms
my face smells of beauty my hands are embalmed
did I not store the leftover oil for years
with precisely this meeting mirrored in mind?
very still I will lie holding in my glee
so as not to rock the earth on this last lap

dance, raise the dust beloved—why are your eyes so gray?
let friends pick sprays of laurel leaves
and twist green victory garlands all entwined:
no one should sorrow lest the bier be becalmed
for I am yours now picked clean of all disgrace
where wind-softly dolphins orbit in the palms
yours entirely released in the gardens of the night

The Lines Have Fallen unto Me
in Beautiful Places
(Poems from Outside, 1983–2006)

I shall change color
so that life not be an obstacle
but a lying low like the nuptial night
one eye rotating
the sucked white mango stone
to scout for sweet devastation, ah
patiently that soft fire of death
as last word fluttering still from the tongue

—Alfonso Quijada

there is no time

there is no time
time is man's skin
it cracks and crackles and shrinks
in life's passing-by
in the fire of being
telling the hours
then letting them be
in the ever reverberating
moment of silence

in the smoking dance
of the evening star and the midnight sun
in the curl of the leaf
in the dove's swiftly
graceful and fluttered
gesture of dying

there is no time
time is the shooting
comet of recall
strewing heaven with the sparks
of stories no one will ever hear again

time's my love for you
the lizard movements
in your body that come and go
to fill the hollows
with the fire of telling
those many faces of departure

there is no time
just the pulse of the heart
as pain under eye-shells

just the emptied tell-skin
of this poem
splotched and measured
by cancer words of forgetting
like lizard shit

pre-word

the older you become the more silent
  you are
outside in morning sun
light over one shoulder
you read in a book
a knapsack for the night
the wisdom of all uncertainties
(oh, the showdown of the word!)

through heavens the pink hot-air balloon drifts
with tongue of stalking fire
on its way to mountains
you don't hear
and later cicadas go murmur-murmur
to stitch and hem heat's silences with shadows

the hunter's fire-stick barks
in the hill of the fox
and the boar and the frog and the rabbit
so rapidly death jumps up
with mute cry
of life's anguish flared in eyes
soon to fade

you cock an ear now
the world is no longer about
the long dance of life with wife
with child with choir of words
with old dog patiently watching the yard

until you are ripe enough to eat—
everything wonderful
white and merciful
    to lose

listen, there's a small bird, somewhere
between peewit and quail,
with duskfall it shoots
two thousand meters high
into the shuttered sky
to while and hood and wink
and wing away
the night on the wind
for its legs are too weak
to sleep on earth
and sometimes it never turns back

I don't understand it either

tonight with moon against slope of darkness
a cold stone cheek
you look into the mirror appearances
of uncertain eternities
and see the sheet
a knapsack of day
the rictus of the old word-fool

and slip away in ashes of duration
and the dog's noise of blackness
to lip-touch the nothing-eye stillness-lie
as pre-word prayer to whiteness

self-portrait

That's me third from the end
just left of center
(the third as well of my line, for I am
my grandfather's grandchild and my father's son
and my mother had a generous mouth),
with the hands of someone who in times gone by
often clutched a hat behind the back.
My eyes are not blue.

I was too young to join
Durruti of the good adventure's
anarchist brigade, and Alexander died
long before my birth, even though he lived again
by mouth of the historians. Is the orifice of speech
indeed the birth-vault of dust?
There's nothing much to tell
about my underpants.

At night dreams enter the houses where I sleep.
Sometimes I converse with flies about suns
and the sins of being human, for I engrave
self-portrait journeys in scattered verses
and align my life to the lines of landscapes.

The person whose yacht capsized
off the coast of Tierra del Fuego
is not me; in fact, I've never yet
seen a live volcano

even if the tongue courts spewing fire.
There are tiny hairs on my hands.

It's someone else who can translate
all the words of *La Traviata* into German.
Nelson Mandela does not count me
among his close hangers-on.
I seldom use lipstick but do sometimes grimace
like an orangutan with toothache in a mirror dulled by breath.
I have a cock between the legs, and say again:
from the urn of my mother I was born,
from her thighs, in blood and distress
and crowing up a noise.

Years ago I wore a number seven shoe
and also believed in the equality of all people,
and listened to the turbid tales of canaries
in cages in the corridors of dark cities.
Look, I'm the man who knows a shopkeeper
with a beauty spot on the nose: after all,
I do make drawings of memory's cellars and inscriptions.

The smell of horses does not take me by the throat.
Sometimes the traffic light turns red against me.
On occasion I've fingered a pornographic photo,
her buttocks were somewhat fleshy and shone
under the oiliness of fingertips.
God does not talk to me.
To look is to create.

That's me, thus my life.

wind silence

it is going to be tough
to forsake this earth
(but who or what goes away?)
the terrible spaces of dispossession
always yours alone

dark hill over there
like a bowl of shimmering light
with trees still bearing the signs of wind
in joint and wound and miracle of breath,
and here a mudslide
slopes and plains
and black vegetation

all suffering is distance—
how could you know of people in the mud?
what is lived? what seen, heard
or merely imagined,
and what matters?

when walls crumble
and the unimpeded cry
opens in you
a pealing, shimmering incantation
of dancing spaces—
a wind silence

where is my love

in a big room behind a glass wall,
looking out above water
the color of green oblivion,
how ferryboats waddle from the quay
to fog-written islands in the bay

mirrored in a pane, the vague figure
of a naked man as he waits.
now and then the veil blows away
and a bone city on a distant mountain coast
flickers fleetingly,
flits and flattens again
to an imagined memory

where is my love my love

on either side the soaring gray metropolis
of concrete and shine and neon thoughts,
along streets the trees in a still
fire of fall,
a few cars, soundless and wet,
sometimes a pedestrian with a mouth of cold breath,
a dog on a leash,
a crow flutters by and later a gull,

storied debates about the nature of being
and what will man be held to account for,
the rush of voices
as the heart bears its shout

where is my love my love

on the edge of this continent
of forest and snow
by the end of the world
at the hem I say
of a dark ocean
where whale-fish roam
to hollowly sound their despair
in waterlogged waiting rooms

if one were to let darkness flood
who would identify the corpse
who fold the shroud like a wing around absence
what name as solitary password
will be pinned to the waterlogged heart's hollow
a crow flies by and later a gull

where is my love oh where is she now

—*Vancouver*

picture

the heart turns over
for the other side
shows a picture
whose elucidation
is written on the front

you live in that darkling drawing
of meaning, woman
woman eternally beloved
since time and forgetting
just beyond the reach of reach

when I know
I don't see
that's when I keep moving
but sometimes you lie silent and empty
in the hollow of my chest

and I rejoice
because repletion is then the finger
that draws the pleated contours of your absence

Rimbaud's journey

when they had to carry Rimbaud
in a litter for three hundred kilometers
from the desert city where hyenas
even in the brightness of noon
snort-laugh and cough outside
the protecting wall,
to the Sea of Reeds
where he hoped to board
a steamer headed for France
to have the rotten leg amputated

when the leg was bloated as big
and gleet-yellow as a spongy gourd
and each little bump or knock
had him laughing and coughing and hiccuping from pain

the bearers had to put him down
on hard earth for the night
and with utmost exertion he then ass-shifted
a foot to the side to claw
with raw fingers a hollow in the ground
in which to shit
and cover with clods
the excretion like a dead poem
as underground sign
for the road back through the maze

on one occasion some camels wandered off
among thorn trees and specters and spurted lightning

so that everybody had to go in search
and under seething skies
the bearers left him swaddled in rags
like a corpse forgotten on its way to the hole

then clouds obliterated the glimmer
and for sixteen hours Rimbaud
with his face turned to the vomiting rain
for deliverance from above
laughed and sobbed and guffawed

New York, September 12, 2001

"Then it went dark. Real dark. Like snow."
—words of a survivor

will the hand endure moving over this paper
will any poem have enough weight
to leave a line of flight above the desolate landscape
ever enough face to lift against death's dark silence
who will tell today

the huge anthill of people remains quiet
somber and bright but obscure
as if the brown effluvium of sputtering towers
sweeps still the skyline with a filthy flag
who will weep today

today images wail for voice behind the eyes
planes as bombs stuffed with shrapnel of soft bodies
then the fire inferno flame-flowers from skyscrapers
human flares like falling angels from the highest floor
down, down all along shimmering buildings of glass and steel
fluted in abandoned beauty and fluttering
weightless and willowy and flame-winged to streamline
fleeting reflections in the fugitive language of forgetting
the hellhound of destruction has a red tongue of laughter

who will tell and who will count
gouged eyes do not understand the blue of sky
through a dismal and chilly nuclear winter
people stumble people shuffle
stumble-people shuffle-people worm-white-people

where lie the faces
old before their end or their wedding
grayed in ashes from head to toe
as if clothed in coats of the snowing knowing of ages

beneath rummage and debris rosy corpses move and mumble
and in East River confidential files and folders float
with shreds and feathers lacerated human meat
scorched confetti for the dog's feast
who will tell tomorrow tomorrow

where are the faces
will the tongue still think
still pulse its dark lair
with flamed memory of bliss
will words still drink oblivion
will any poem some day ever carry sufficient weight
to leave the script of scraps recalling fall and forgetting

will death remain quivering in the paper

the ashes and us

it is the tree-coolness by day
like a robe of grace
draped around the trunk
it is the fire by night
burning holes in the dark
it is where sun and moon perish
and the answerableness
of identity
is weighed slaked shifted
to all evil things worded away
not-us is the fulcrum of rancor

in squatting together for solace
memory is leisurely fumbled
folded fashioned
measure by measure
and fitted to words
do we know who we are
one by one
for you and one
for me the blood and the clay
the rememberer's song

but when the tree is chopped down
so that sun burns a stain in the eye
and fire goes to ashes
to a scorched blot of absence
we are strewn to four winds

do I not know who I am
wandering through the flame-fed day
and night's shivering articulations
looking for you as if for a mirror

the communist remembers

fall: and advent of the colder season
with smoldering skylines
summer dreams of revolt and peace
career through remembrances
are dead spiders on paper

trapped on Tower City's sidewalks
in brightness mirrored by glass cliffs
where clouds cavort
(the little sun man shrinks smaller by the day)
old Chinese ladies with dead eyelids sit
cross-legged in blackout
to protest the torturing of Falun Gong
yellow cabs cruise; a flash of sounds
resonates wall to wall through ravines
from shrubs in the park protrude
the scabbed ankles and torn feet of a drifter

with darkness the city is a surging heart
of veiled passions and sleepless regrets
a whirl of white moths each the size
of this waving hand glitters and whorls
and fists in blue-pillared searchlights
scanning the nocturnal space
above the gap where heaven-lurching
skyscrapers of capitalism once soared
and now but a pool of lost thoughts
helicopters twirl like moths from hell

above the somber copse of chimneys and spires
and shoot light-beams on roof and garden and lane

who ever promised you a hollow for your foot?
who knew all belief must lead to slaughter?
who could suspect that conscience is but a crease
of forgetting within smoldering skylines?

when fire chariots cease lowing
and the moon blossoms strangely
and screens flicker their silent news of war
in the lodges of slumbering doormen
you crouch on the sill
to track the wakening of gull and crow

one eye peeled for the swathe
of first light sweeping the East River
like the memory of another distant land's
summer dreams of uprising and peace
still signaling in the dead tongue
the green pastures of your past
the flat-roofed houses, reeds, a wind and smoke

and when the glimmer is sheer
you again notice your hands
already the color of moldy pumpkin
(the little sun man shrinks smaller by the day)
and *know* that spider's blood over pale paper tells
thus your dying word by word,
to reconcile death's wonder-making

the cup of words

when it was night I rose from the bed
to look for the ocean's white movements,
you still asleep then between last night and morrow,
sea mews were stitching dark wounds to words
as I stuttered these thoughts

what is the gist of the slow twisting heart?
is memory but pulsating fiction
wrapped as an eye in night's sluggish paper schooner
to be fistballed on this ocean of departure?

how far the road we traveled together,
lights in the trees,
you a sleek leopard by my side
while the hand moved over silences and steeps

we knocked on five thousand doors of this keep
and you always there to steady my fingers
when the sorrow of letters started to tremble,
you made of my body a slow holy city

faraway countries, distant horizons,
sounds of piano, a paper of nations,
wings in your hair and birds in your dreams,
the golden glow of Spain,
orange walls of island verandas,
and precipitously too-livid towers tongue-fired,
flaming thorn trees over endless savannas

the apricot moon on beaches of milk
where purple-spiraled shells sing of the sea,
and elsewhere a sun poem bursting
silk, the way cornfields break a skyline,
but forever the lilting weight of your hands
a fluted glass at my lips

these words will stalk and stubble the pages,
this burning sea sing the shelling of ages
in foam and in kelp
and the ancient fruit of the moon,
your visage, your face
a cup for my dreams of far destinations

the shame of stations,
prisons, a littering list
of names
and shadows and shades
and gallows and dates and knuckles,
the five thousand shuttered phonemes of passion,
and shawls and shackles
as snails over the eye

when it was night still I stood by the window
looking for the ocean's white news of day,
you on guard somewhere between flying
away and arrival,
and I was afraid

but now morning breaks,
and now you are young,

this then your day of birds,
once again your song

take along the nightbread of your lover
as a wordfool's breakfast
with condiments sweet regret and contentment
in celebration of your hours,
my beloved

my beloved, my beloved,
may the sun bone this heaven an eternity of blue,
may this mountain's mercy cover your fears
with silence against the shrieking of water
and the hollows of stuttered shadows

yea, may the majesty of this mountain watch over you
and bring succor,
and the primordial leopard laughter of living

the oath

if ever my hands forget
the rounding of your body
the hollows and the curves
and your smooth warm skin—
may they swell and burst like cantaloupes
may ants devour them at night
when I lie sheathed in my sheet
may they rot in earth's obscurity

if ever my eyes forget
the come-and-go of your breath
the contractions of your spine in love
the long descending slip of your belly—
may the hoarse crows snip them at noon
may they drown in blindness as if in milk
may boys use them as marbles to roll
on the village square when shadows are blue

if ever my cock forgets the magic
lining of your cunt
the deepmount and the roselip clitoris
and the throbbing big-make of your voice—
may it wither then like a dead fig shoot
may it be mute like a mouthfool without tongue
may a dog swallow it inadvertently
and shit it out on the beach

and should my heart ever forget
the touch of your hands

betray the surge of your hair
not recall the receptive opening of your thighs—
may it be pierced by the executioner's blade
may it stifle in the red flood of blood
may it rage with pain down the ages
for then I have never known your heart
for then I have lived in vain
and death will show me too much clemency

embark

A giant albino with wide teeth
   controlled my passport:
"You speak French with an accent, sir?"
"I speak all languages with an accent, sir."
"Oh. Happy Christmas."

Christmas Eve. The shepherd star shines warm
   in the dark African night.
"A Savior is born
in distant Bethlehem . . ."
my people sang.
They are all dead,
long since worn to a shine and forgotten
like memory food
under the warm blue African earth.

On board the nearly empty aircraft
some drunken soldiers sing.
We will fly through dark times
with under the wings dead countries,
the dead words of freedom dreams.

And I lie back and think of you,
beloved, close under eyelids. We will fly
through dark times, beloved. I will dream you
like an immaculate beloved knowledge.

Goree hours

Six o'clock
when sun tarnishes the sea
with silver coin
you go swim in the thick warm water;
from night, from a shed of darkness
the first pirogue returns to the island
like something striving to break from the womb;
fishermen sit bolt upright in the bottom
and listen to the call for first prayers
and then the land as well is fingered
by the glittering reflections of living death;
on the small beach white pigeons peck
wary of the outcast cats, come here
to bury their excretion
while waiting for a portion cast-away fish
from the depths of night;
afterward the blowflies gather brilliantly
around fish heads that could not be devoured;
and you return to the walled-off patio
where it's still cool
    and the frangipani's fleshy petals,
torn loose by night's warm wind
like fragrant shards strewn over the tiles,
will remember the wedding

dancing with D at Celra's village festival

tonight when for the first time
you accompanied me in borrowed heels
to the ball
my heart was a little burnt-out cigar
in my breast
with dead smoke and stale regret
sweet on the lips

I must still bend slightly
with a hand on your back   your back
nearly that of a young woman
now   you and I alone
as I take you through the dancers
how long before your dark pearled eye
will be flattered and captured
by the strutting steps of other prancers?

only yesterday you were wet on my lap,
or did I carry you in my arms,
on the floor   and the many questions,
all those poems I had to recap;
you wanted to learn the universe's song
and then your plait came undone to bloom
in a fragrant bouquet

I still wanted to stop: tell you
life is not worth the music they play
and now it's too late
                    what does
an old man's heart know of smoke anyway?

tonight on my chest one last tango
under the town square's dripping stars and folderol
against a naked sky
when the outgrown moon strikes twelve
we step out on your first *paso doble*

you with the blushed heels of first love
but with fire,
I the bittersweet dead heart
in the mouth.

to empty the mountain
for Wang Wei

Halfway through life's journey I discover the Way
Wind fleet-footed, heavens still, long-armed monkeys crying.
Now that I'm old I live near green mountains,
Water so clear and sand so white,
Backwards the birds fly
I wander alone there
And with no mouth-companion enjoy unfolded silence.
The endless river rolls its waves hour upon hour
But cannot bring to heel the moon;
After my long illness I scale the heights;
Loitering to where the stream sinks in moss
I rest and watch how clouds appear;
Passing on, I meet the old neighbor
And forget to return and chatter above and below
In one moving sand of words: Oh, we live in desperate times
And mourn our hair of snow
Squeezed by poverty, we even give up the wine!

winter work

when you get up the house
is dug from the night
truculent and cold like a tomb /
the day outside is clean and stiff
north the mountain chain
a clear shot
endless white reverberation of snow
where angels with iced wings
spurt from the void / time's
color is not that of heaven
the old monk said
as he fell in love with the nun

language is not the cloth of meaning /
there is no deep knowledge which
when unwrapped must be gutted and debunked /
mystery already whispers
in the surface movements

on the land now the trees are emptied
last year's pruned branches
and dry weeds put to fire /
in the silent cold the flame is directly
an orange flutter-tongue whispered from the sods /
it might have been the pyre
of a madwoman's bygone life

no chirp of bird in the wide vicinity /
no winging refugee

to do the rounds
or carry knowledge of flight to the eye /
just time clotting to die
without a robe of celestial hue

later you chuck the cherry-tree trunk
thick as a thigh on the tame hearth inside
and stare at the crackling tongues
while dew descends like darkness
on the house / something
smells of sweet nun's fig

the hand a blind chameleon
tiptoeing from vowel to sound
made speechless because the sum
of walking is so long since gone

("the poem is a fragrant flower
with the spots of a leopard
polished by endless boning
and written in the ink of two centuries")

—*Can Ocells*

Goya

Francisco de Goya y Lucientes
with candles on the brim of his hat
straddles the rim of a dark century dark horses
my beloved
mouth-blind and the scream of terror
a dead stone in the head the head
of a dog squinting over earth's hump

and inscribes his black paintings
on plaster of house walls the house
of the deaf masks under a rotten
rolling moon
my beloved

black as blood
black as bread
black as murder
black as chaos
black as execution
white like the fire flashing from the muzzle
of the gun
the bull smothers in his own blood
life is quicklime muffling the bones

from dark heaven arises a carnival
of cripples condemned ones a flare
of ghosts his hand remembers
does the hand still remember
the fawning of idiot king and retarded princesses

the bayonet in the freedom fighter's gut
the crowning of the sardine remember
still the slender outline
the pale flesh and the dark fleece
of Maria del Pilar Teresa Cayetana
de Silva Alvarez de Toledo
la Duquesa de Alba
my beloved

his *maja* in red and black and gold
dark horses in the night the night
a *populacho* in procession
black like insomnia
our god is a mule
a muted blinding cry
a wall of darker fire

it is said poetry completes
what history leaves out
black like death
my beloved
my beloved

I'm so glad we live in peaceful times

lookback

I too
I too danced
heard the music over the hills
quiver like shaken sky
how the hand leaves its unreadableness on the wall
I deciphered fires in the night
got to frequent love intimately
found the broken-winged god in a book
traveled from tavern to woman to understanding
to mountaintop ecstasy
when the world folded in eternity
and the sun was a moon
and the sun was a singing moon

I also
I also saw how the human is skinned
brandished a fist against the sky
learned how to spell through blue lips
the heart is a rotted dark fruit
had to listen how children with torn-off limbs
howl in their throats
I came across women wrinkled like ancient desert bags
with dead infants at the tit
thought history carried exact meaning
or an eye at least
and saw the snake of obsequiousness suck
the ass of power
slitheringly shiny like a conscience

and the sun was a moon
and the sun was a bloody moon

I too
I also wandered through looking glasses
when aircraft ignited the towers as pyres
how my father was hanged with a grin in the door
and my beloved in the bitterly flowering bush
I also fought the dog for meat
also heard my voice murmuring verse in a hollow cavern
like the white lies of the rapist
like the superstitious prayers of the hypocrite
I also saw my face disappear
and how my body like a worn coat
without protection against cold will forget time
and again
how the sun is a moon
a silent, chilly moon

in a cab in the rain, New York

women are raising pale arms
in the smoking damp air
to hail taxis—

rain shivers like fountains from a mountain
trickling down the glass walls of celestial towers—
fishes jump clear of the river
of paintings held captive in museums—
my dream is a city of one million dwellings
and beckoning roads to unexplored lands—

listen, all you need to take is a lipstick
and I two bottles of wine—
and we will wake from the darkened stream
of deep traveling
on a luminous bed in a singular inn
with the pale gurgling of water in the gutters—

so that I may drunkenly utter—
no, write in red on the misty mirror:
I love you, you know—
yes, yes I now love you so

the meeting

when my heart comes to me
through the night
the streets where horse carts go
clip-clopping to collect black bags
of trash
are fragrant with fallen flowers
from the frangipani trees

when my heart comes to me
through the night
I set a table by the window
with bread and wine and sweet
dark figs

and write this little poem
as a full-blown paper moon
of waiting
to echo that other of white stone
outside
traveling the night
where dark men drive their horses

when my heart comes to me
through the night
when the waiting is filled

with words
we'll eat the figs and drink the wine
and make love to the moon

—*Porto Alegre*

for Juan Carvajal

the flesh of whores is mournful
I saw them waiting
with the dark ejaculation between thighs
along the boulevard giving
hem and hail to the sea
under a heaven of stars
like dead fish

the flesh of whores is sad
I saw them lie naked
in the words and the hands
of poets and painters
trying to keep
death alive
things are the purloined
meaning of things

I sat in the garden
and heard the piercing ejaculation
of the parrot in the palm tree
and the sorrowfulness of life
grew in me
like a dark fruit
like a whore heart

—Tampico, November 3, 2003

this is the season

this is the season when the dreamer,
swathed in dark remembrances
like an infant swaddled in the weavings of night,
often sobs in his sleep

this is the season when he finds a copper coin
under stripped trees in the lane,
the bankrupt moon, a rusted leaf,
the barking dog,
and precipitously the heart tumbles
and memory brings back
widgeons in the reed-bush,
crackling evenings,
waves combed in tresses on the beach,
your beautiful hips
a violin with a scroll at heaven's door
for the tongue to enter your bliss

awareness is a boat nosing for the open sea
and life a body slithering over its side,
sinking like a sob
to wash up tomorrow among rocks
for the postmortem opening-up
in search of meaning

when the moon is full of rot
I shall go to Santiago de Cuba
I shall go to Santiago
in a carriage of black water

this is the season when church bells peal
and snow must slip over towers and spires and peaks
silence shroud the hollows of the city
like cold come from heaven

Estos dias, iguales a otros dias de otros años:
these days exactly like the days of earlier years
with people exactly like those of then
with the same hours and the dead
with similar desires
and the old-old restlessness of before
is *here*

nothing happens
you're not alone
with the sleepless cold, you come
you go, you don't know where
or why

put on angel wings, love,
and I'll suck my tongue
while playing the violin
in a carriage of black water

it's not so terrible leaving the battle dishonorably

"porque en mi corazon viven tus besos como banderas rojas"
—*Pablo Neruda*

when night wiped out the view of mountainsides
like smog over the barrios
of extreme poverty
and vultures in darkness above the city
had to swerve their flight fumbling
down the polluted sky,
I danced with her,
saw her dress blow like a bell,
the flash of her red shoes over the floor

we drank two bottles of heavy Argentinean wine,
in a wordless undertaking she admitted me
to her room
and took me in her bed

and gradually the streets' growling dimmed,
the poor make a city so ugly and black,
in mildewed offices behind barred windows
the torturers' arms became heavy
from ask-and-hit and hit-and-ask

all through the hours I dreamed I was asleep
with open eyes,
her breathing next to me so peaceful and deep

and when the first lights flickered on the mountain
like the cigarette coals of those
due for execution at dawn
and vultures flapped heavily in their quest
for an early draft up, up and away,
I covered her again,
and when she sighed with fluttering eyelids
I asked, "What's your name?"

"Death," she said,
"my name is Death,"
while her seed as warm as blood
flooded and fertilized my belly and my thighs
with the odors of birth

the way back

then Wordfool told the woman and the child
come let us squat on our haunches
                    here against the climb
and look down on the smoking city
to take stock—
we remain tied to the road
as the place of origin
even though we've forgotten the people's names

then Wordfool told the woman and the child
we are free
I know it is hard
and once every year it is good
to turn around
and look back
on the journeys and the state of the dead

once every year
the season goes dark
and the time is right
and ripe to bring the pumpkin
a celestial fruit of eternal life
to market

come let us sing

how shall we preserve the flesh?
in crypts mummies nod their heads

heavy with the travels of decay
moths and blight darken their coats with holes

how shall we exorcise distance?
we stuff the trips and the tides
with desert honey and locust meat
and forgotten remembrances of the Old Country—
that a good fragrance may come from the hills
and keep book in the dust

then Wordfool told the woman and the child
let's imagine ourselves as scouts
gather wood and light the fire
to signal to the dwellers
of the dead city
that we wish to entice the moon
                from her dark hollows
to reconcile with the pumpkin

moreover Wordfool told the woman and the child
forgive me please
one makes poems also from sticks and seeds
to capture the soft words
one is always looking for measure and rhyme
and then the combustion of incarnation
you mustn't tell anybody

for Michael Fried: Paris, December 21, 2004

we live in dark times
birds of heaven are poisoned
we roam through brightly lit halls
stare myopically at exhibitions
of gray imaginaries, encyclopedias of passing
meticulously annotated absences of sense

the emptier the contents the more painfully
perfection and the perfidy of looking will flow
as the world completes itself through us
and we see corpse camps, genocide, man
abjuring his skein of belonging
in a desperate wing-beat to be
free of death
the birds of heaven are poisoned
and we live in dark times

and somewhere on fetid waters of holy rivers
burning effigies of dark-faced goddesses bob
they've long since stopped singing to us

in closet spaces we stare myopically
at the skinned life of the writer
naked like a soft dragon on the floor
to kiss a black tongue to the shoe
of his cruel beloved
the spine a curve of cursed words
and we see death camps, genocide, troughs
stuffed with corpses, man

jeering at his rope of legitimacy
in a thrashing wing-thrust
to be free of passing
has long since stopped singing to us

"finally, when I shave my somber morning face
I have the impression of shaving
my cadaver before it is put on its bier
and let to water
in the putrid river of oblivion"

from the void comes incarnation
comes dark wind
will the wind be a wound
and signal the blind child

in twilit cellar chambers
we eat salad and lard and bread
suddenly recall the stories of illicit ancestors
how clumsily our mouths fold around deceased tongues
to elicit murmurs of forgetting
man relinquishes the illumination
of ever again being mad and clear

and out there the clear city rises
magnificent ruin of man's monstrous imagination
where much love was committed
and murders often done by knife
while the writer sang
of incandescent rivers where goddesses bathe
the water dragon naked and blind

to the left a high moon slips
as petrified subconsciousness
chafed pale by dust of space and time

tomorrow paper snow will litter and letter
the roof-map and the nest of streets
and from gutters icy drops will drip
on dark faces of shivering wanderers

the blood on the doorposts

old poet
come
break the unleavened bread
take the water
let it be your meal of enlightenment

you ask:
watchman on the city's walls,
judge of our unnumbered hours,
when will the day fall open again?

know then
somewhere else it is always bright
only you are blind
and the shadows clogging our world
are hills
are birds

as the crab bursts from its carapace
let your cancer blossom free
throw up your soul
take your own death
for whiter than snow
whiter still than the break of day
your blood will wash you

come
be passover lamb
give me your blunted hand

bend down
recognize the final black rose
and say
to hell with the whole damned lot
and die free of your fears

because poet
I'll pile stones on your moon bed
as white as verse
whiter still than the markers of your journey
so the poisonous rains of dusk
do not discolor your bones
so that birds from the hills
do not choke on your worms

old poet
come
smear blood on the doorposts
your deliverance is at hand
make song